COLONIAL PEOPLE

The Merchant

WENDY MEAD

Cavendish
Square
New York

Published in 2014 by Cavendish Square Publishing, LLC
303 Park Avenue South, Suite 1247, New York, NY 10010

Website: cavendishsq.com

This publication represents the opinions and views of the author based on his or her personal experience, knowledge, and
research. The information in this book serves as a general guide only. The author and publisher have used their best efforts in
preparing this book and disclaim liability rising directly or indirectly from the use and application of this book.

CPSIA Compliance Information: Batch #WS13CSQ

All websites were available and accurate when this book was sent to press.

Library of Congress Cataloging-in-Publication Data

Mead, Wendy.
The merchant / Wendy Mead.
p. cm. — (Colonial people)
Includes bibliographical references and index.
Summary: "Explores the life of a colonial merchant and his importance to the community, as well as everyday life
responsibilities, and social practices during that time"—Provided by publisher.
ISBN 978-1-60870-415-6 (hardcover) — ISBN 978-1-62712-047-0 (paperback) — ISBN 978-1-60870-986-1 (ebook)
1. Merchants—United States—History—17th century—Juvenile literature. 2. Merchants—United States—History—18th
century—Juvenile literature. 3. United States—Social life and customs—To 1775—Juvenile literature. 4. United States—
History—Colonial period, ca.1600-1775—Juvenile literature. I. Title. II. Series.
HF3025.M48 2013
381.0973—dc23
2011028343

Editor: Peter Mavrikis
Art Director: Anahid Hamparian
Series Designer: Kay Petronio

Photo research by Marybeth Kavanagh

Cover photo by Bettmann/CORBIS

The photographs in this book are used by permission and through the courtesy of:
North Wind Picture Archives: 4, 9, 11, 14, 27, 36, 41, 42; *Alamy*: brt PHOTO, 7; Irene Abdou, 19; John Elk III, 30;
Bettmann/Corbis, 32; *The Colonial Williamsburg Foundation*: 16, 21, 24, 25; *The Image Works*: akg-images, 39

Printed in the United States of America

CONTENTS

ONE

Supplies for a New Life

In the biggest town in the **colony,** the streets teem with people. A woman walks to buy cloth. A farmer carts in some crops. He hopes to sell the crops so that he can get some sugar. They may both find what they need by visiting a **merchant,** a person who buys and sells things. Merchants help make life easier for those starting over in a new land.

Beginning in the early 1600s, England established colonies in North America. By the middle of the century, the English government passed laws to help manage the economy of the mother country and its colonies. In this economic system, the mother country obtained raw materials and agricultural products in exchange for finished products for sale to the colonists. This system was known as **mercantilism**. People in England and parts of Europe left their homes to start a

Colonists gather in the streets of Philadelphia.

new life. Some came voluntarily with means to build a farm or plantation. Others agreed to sell their labor for a number of years in exchange for the cost of their passage. They were called **indentured servants**. The English government also allowed prisoners and debtors to be sold into indentured labor in the colonies against their will. They sailed across the Atlantic Ocean where they helped create the thirteen colonies of British America. These colonies were ruled by England until 1776.

These newcomers had great hopes for their new homes. Some wanted to be allowed to practice their religion freely. Others thought they could achieve great wealth. Many English men, women, and children were sold into indentured servitude against their will. All faced the challenge of building homes and establishing businesses and farms. Many of the colonists turned to merchants to supply all the items they needed to achieve their dreams.

Trade in the Colonies

Merchants performed an important job in colonial times. They helped bring in tools and other items from England to the colonies and shipped out local products such as fur, tobacco, rice, and lumber to sell abroad. Merchants traded with other countries, too.

Merchants brought in **goods** from other countries such as silk, sugar, wine, and even slaves.

Trade also took place between the colonies. Northern colonists traded molasses and rum manufactured from Caribbean sugar for the much-valued tobacco found on southern colonial farms called **plantations**. Merchants also took orders for goods and sent requests to other merchants and traders in England.

Merchants sell many items, including soap, flour, and meat.

Besides supplying goods, merchants acted as a bank of sorts. They bought extra crops from farmers, giving them **credit** at their store in return. The credit could be used at a later time to buy goods from the merchant. Merchants may have also **bartered** with other colonists. For example, a merchant would accept homemade yarn in exchange for some sugar or tea.

Merchants also helped the colonists get the latest news. Working with other merchants in London, colonial merchants could get the latest information on the events back in England. They also had copies of English newspapers and other publications sent over. Merchants received letters from their business partners and listened to stories from the ship captains who delivered their goods to the colonies.

A Family Affair

Many colonial merchants had strong ties to those already in the business in England. They often started out working for brothers, cousins, and in-laws back home, serving as their **factor**, or representative, in the colonies. It would be their job to help sell items brought over by boat and buy goods to refill merchant ships for their trip back. A factor also collected money owed to the merchant for products sold.

Read All About It!

In the 1600s, colonists did not have any local newspapers. They often relied on merchants and travelers for information. The first colonial newspaper started in Boston in 1704. About twenty-five years later, colonists had thirteen newspapers to choose from. These publications printed stories about events in London. Other articles covered news on the latest ships that were arriving or leaving **port**.

Merchants used newspapers to let people know what items they had to sell. One advertisement in the May 23, 1771, issue of the *Virginia Gazette* read:

Just **IMPORTED** from London . . . and to be SOLD . . . in Norfolk. . . . European Goods. . . . Also on Hand . . . Rum . . . Sugar . . . which we will sell cheap, for cash or . . . credit. LOGAN, GILMOUR, and Company

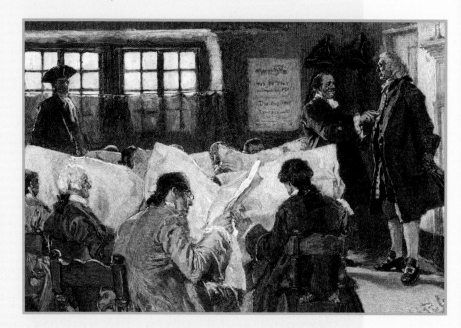

Because they needed people they could trust, merchants relied mainly on relatives and friends. A merchant's business usually stayed within a family, with all the accounts and goods being passed down through the generations. Arriving in Northampton, Massachusetts, in 1660, David Wilton became one of the town's leading merchants. His grandson-in-law Joseph Hawley took over the business after Wilton's death. Hawley's son, Joseph Hawley II, then ran the family operation for a time, and so did his two sons.

Money Matters

In early colonial times, merchants focused mostly on four products: fish, fur, lumber, and tobacco. They made money from the many natural resources found in their new homeland. Fish, fur, lumber, and tobacco became their most popular early products. They sold these items to merchants back in England.

Often the colonial merchant received credit instead of money for his goods sold abroad. This credit often took the form of a **bill of exchange**, a special type of letter. This letter asked one person to pay someone for the goods another person bought. For example, John Norton had a large trading business in both Virginia and London. He and his son wrote to each other and included bills of exchange in their messages.

In some cases, merchants wanted some quick form of payment. They accepted different types of gold and silver coins, including **pieces of eight** from Spain. Paper money and coins, however, were in short supply. So they had to be creative about how they were paid for their goods.

Early colonists also traded with the American Indians for land and goods. Indians were interested in glass and metal goods for their reflective quality, but quickly prized them

Merchants trade goods for animal pelts with American Indians.

for their usefulness. They traded for pots, knives, and guns in exchange for food, land, and animal pelts and hides that the English demanded. Merchants supplied the goods for the Indian trade, sold the land and food they purchased to other colonists, and sold the pelts and hides back to **tanners** and clothiers in England.

Merchants used the English money system for their prices. They wrote down the symbol £ to represent the pound sterling. It is called "sterling" because it started out as a coin made from sterling silver. Each pound equaled 20 shillings, which was marked as "s." Each shilling could be broken down into 12 pence. Merchants used the abbreviation "d." for pence. Even if they received payment in goods, not silver, they would record the value of the payment in pounds, shillings, or pence.

TWO

The Shop and the Ship

In the merchant's kitchen, logs burn brightly in the fireplace. Steam escapes from an iron kettle, or pot, hanging over the fire. Inside the kettle the merchant finds a warm, comforting mush made from corn. He scoops some out into a bowl with a metal spoon. The merchant eats his breakfast and washes it down with a drink of cider from a cup. Shipped across the ocean, the kettle, spoon, and cup are just a few of the prized goods that the merchant got from overseas.

With a full belly, the merchant puts on his beaver-skin hat and walks out the door. His first stop of the morning will be his shop. He owns one of the buildings on the town's main street near the waterfront.

Walking down a cobblestone street, the merchant approaches his shop. The store is filled with all kinds of goods, from tea to tools to the latest fashions from England.

Here colonists could buy iron pots and pans as well as coffee and spices. They also could get nails, hammers, and other tools needed to build their homes and tend to their farms. To feed their families, the colonists turned to the merchant for flour, sugar, and meat. Many merchants sold a lot of rum, too.

Merchants also sold cloth. Some colonists made their own fabric from locally grown flax and linen. But this process took a lot of time. Those who could afford it often bought linen, wool, cotton, or silk fabric woven in England.

A colonist cooks for her family using iron tools.

Taking Care of Business

The merchant visits his **counting room** at the shop. This is a separate room where he oversees his business. The merchant keeps track of the customers' purchases by writing them down in an account book. He lets some of his customers have credit at his shop, or permits them to buy the goods now and pay for them later. Sometimes people did not pay the merchant back for the items they bought. Merchants had to keep this problem in mind when making up prices for the supplies in their store. They also added in the cost of shipping when setting the price for an item.

The merchant's son works as his clerk, or assistant. His son helps out with the account book and any bills or letters that the merchant needs to have written. The clerk also keeps track of all the materials in the merchant's warehouse where he stores some of his goods.

Working with other merchants living thousands of miles away presents special challenges. The merchant writes lots of letters trying to manage his business deals. He informs another merchant about shipping delays. In another letter, the merchant lists the items he wants to buy. Merchants on both sides of the Atlantic act as "middlemen" in the trade between the producers of raw materials and the manufacturers and consumers of

Merchants sometimes received paper money and coins as payment.

finished products. They make their profit by obtaining, transporting, and delivering demanded products.

The merchant's factor in the West Indies would write to him to let him know how much rice to obtain to sell to sugar planters and would offer advice about other items to send next time, such as American-made footwear or cheap "homespun" cloth for slave clothing. West Indian sugar was the most valuable agricultural product in the British Empire, and the American farmers, tradesmen, and merchants supplied the sugar planters with all they needed to grow the crop. The merchants purchased the sugar and sold it to refiners in Massachusetts to make molasses, sugar cones, and rum. Merchants then took these products to sell in England, where they would purchase furniture, silverware, and clothing. A clerk would keep records of orders and transactions in letter books so that the merchant could review them later. The merchant might ask the clerk to send out several copies of the same letter. Letters could take weeks to arrive and sometimes got lost.

Gathering Goods

After checking on his store, the merchant walks over to his warehouse down on the wharf. Here he keeps a lot of the goods that he is preparing to send out for **export**, or shipment out of the country, to England. He owns slaves and indentured servants who manage the flow of goods, and when there is extra work, he hires day laborers for a wage to load and unload his **cargo**. In addition to selling goods to the town's residents, the merchant also ships supplies to England and other places to trade. The merchant has some wooden poles, or masts, made from trees found in the area. He knows that London merchants prize the tall masts made in the colonies.

The merchant also has rice, cheap clothing, knives, tools, sugar, rum, wooden beams, and planks that he plans to sell to a sugar plantation owner in the British West Indies. With the money from that sale, the merchant's agent will buy sugarcane, to be sent back to the colonies. Molasses, a by-product from the process of making sugar from the sugarcane, was popular because it is used as an ingredient in making rum. The merchant's agent

Life of a Merchant Woman

Most merchants were men, but some women helped out with their family's businesses. A few found success in buying and selling goods on their own.

Margaret Hardenbroeck, a successful merchant, moved to the colony of New Amsterdam in 1659. She had grown up in a merchant family in Amsterdam, Holland. She first worked for her merchant cousin in New Amsterdam. Her job was to collect debts owed to her cousin and to help sell his goods in the colony. New Amsterdam later became the colony of New York after the English took it over from the Dutch.

Not long after her arrival, Hardenbroeck married a trader named Pieter Rudolphus de Vries. The two worked together and started a family. After de Vries's death in 1660, Hardenbroeck built up their merchant business. She added two new ships to her holdings. These vessels helped her transport goods from Europe to be sold in the colonies. She also used them to carry items to Europe.

Hardenbroeck married Frederick Philipse in 1662. With her new husband's help, she continued to expand her business. Hardenbroeck traded with American Indians for animal skins. A tireless worker, she sometimes traveled on her own ships to make sure the goods arrived safely. On one trip in 1679, she carried cloth, frying pans, books, bricks, and other items from Amsterdam to New York.

Dishware, glasses, and baskets fill the shelves of a merchant's store.

also buys excess slaves from the Caribbean colonies. During the colonial period, more than 200,000 slaves were transported by merchants to the thirteen colonies, the overwhelming majority coming from the millions of slaves those same merchants had imported from Africa to the Caribbean.

In another corner of the warehouse, the merchant keeps barrels of beef and fish. The beef and fish have been dried and salted to keep them from spoiling. The merchant also plans to sell these items on his ship's next trip to the southern colonies.

Goods from Across the Sea

Down on the docks, a merchant's latest ship has arrived from England. He visits the vessel to meet with his **supercargo**, the person who watches over the merchant's goods during the voyage. Sometimes this job is done by the ship's captain. Merchants also hired ship captains to sell their products abroad.

This ship has brought over goods from England. The goods include china dishes, medicines, women's stockings, ribbon, and thread. The merchant will sell some of these items in his store. He may also sell them to other merchants who live further inland. These country storekeepers will resell the items to their customers for a higher price.

With foreign goods, the merchant faces some risks. When he boards the ship, it is the first time he gets to see what he bought. He has to trust that the London merchant had packed the right goods. The merchant also has to believe that the items are in good shape. For any type of food or drink, he worries that they might have spoiled during the trip. Ships always carried rats that nibbled away at a merchant's goods stored on board.

Sometimes foreign merchants sent old or poorly made goods. Virginia merchant Francis Jerdone wrote an angry letter to a London cloth merchant after getting some bad cotton fabric: "I

Workers unload a barrel from a merchant's newly arrived ship.

entreat you to send me more substantial cotton, than what you did last Voyage, for such thin stuff will neither keep out wet or cold."

Selling Goods Abroad

With his ship in port, the merchant must prepare for its next trip. He sometimes needed months to gather up enough items to fill the ship's cargo hold for the journey. The merchant would buy goods from local farmers and merchants in other colonies to stock the ship.

What the merchant picked for the ship depended on where it was going. Merchant Aaron Lopez's ship *Diana* sailed from Newport, Rhode Island, to the island of Jamaica in 1767. On board, he had 10 horses, 103 sheep, 54 turkeys, and 23 geese. Lopez also had 55 barrels of flour, 30 barrels of oil, and 20 barrels of preserved beef. Jamaica and some other Caribbean islands had large sugar plantations. The farmers there, called planters, needed food for themselves and their workers.

In addition to his **wares**, the merchant needed to get supplies for the ship's crew and passengers. An English merchant owned the *Mary*, a ship that often sailed between Philadelphia and London. Roughly sixteen people worked on the ship on its first trip to London. Another thirty-five individuals signed on as passengers. For this trip, the merchant bought five barrels of beef, one barrel of pork, and ten barrels of rum. He also bought some food from a local baker. The ship carried numerous casks full of water as well. These were just some of the food and drinks needed to sustain all the people for the long journey.

THREE

A Man of Many Meetings

Taking a break from his workday, the merchant returns to his home. He sits down to have dinner, which took place in the early afternoon. His wife has prepared a stew for his meal.

In his dish, he can see pieces of pork, corn, squash, and beans. English colonists used few spices in their food. They usually only added salt and pepper. Some seasoned their food with herbs, such as parsley and thyme. They would grow these herbs in their gardens. These gardens also supplied them with parsnips, carrots, and other vegetables.

The merchant enjoys his dinner alone. Colonial families did not always eat together. On Sundays, however, he and his family would share a meal and spend time together. On other days, the merchant might eat with others in the community.

Merchants often met to discuss business, politics, and the news of the day.

Merchants sometimes belonged to local clubs and groups. The Boston merchant John Rowe wrote in his diary that "April 10. The Charitable Society met this day at Mrs. Cordis', and dined, as usual, had a Genteel dinner and twenty three dined there, made choice of officers for the Year."

Back to Business

Later in the day, the merchant stops in at the coffeehouse. Local politicians and businessmen lingered in the rooms there to talk. They might play cards or hold meetings. Just like the coffeehouses in England, these places sold warm drinks, such as coffee, tea, and chocolate, to their customers.

At the coffeehouse, the merchant meets up with other traders. Merchants, especially in large port cities, worked together to bring in and send out goods. They might agree to share the cargo space on an outgoing ship headed toward another colony or another country.

By sharing a ship, no one merchant would lose too much if something happened to it. Merchant ships faced all sorts of hazards. They could be sunk in bad weather. During wars between England and other countries, colonial ships could be taken over by licensed "privateers" from rival governments. And at any time, merchants faced the

Merchants talk business at the coffeehouse.

threat of pirates. These dangerous sailors traveled up and down the coast of the colonies, attacking ships and taking their cargo.

Taxes and Duties

With his ship in the harbor, the merchant next stops at the custom house. He meets with the customs agent to pay **duties**, or fees, on his goods. These fees were charged for bringing certain goods to the colony and for shipping items overseas. These taxes supported the services that enriched the merchants and the nation in the imperial mercantilistic economy. They also ensured that American producers had guaranteed markets to sell their products, and the credit to purchase the manufactured goods they desired.

The customs agent collected these fees for the English government. The English government passed laws about how much to charge the merchants and which of the goods to tax. Some merchants saw benefits to these laws. The laws gave the colonists an easy-to-reach market for their goods. As colonists, they had a special relationship with England. This made it easier for them to borrow money for their businesses. Most colonial merchants operated within the law, but some chose to

A merchant takes a customer to court to get back money owed.

smuggle goods directly to or from other countries to bypass the customs duty. Sometimes the merchants gave money to the customs agent to avoid paying these extra charges. Until 1764, there were no colonial protests or complaints that these duties were unfair.

At the Courthouse

The merchant next walks to the courthouse. The brick building with white shutters stands in the center of town. He pushes open the heavy wooden doors to the courtroom. The merchant has been trying to collect money owed to him by a farmer for some grain, nails, and other supplies. It has been months since the farmer bought the goods. By going to court, the merchant hopes that the farmer will be forced to pay him back.

A panel of judges asks the merchant to tell his side of the story. He explains that the farmer owes him money. Cases involving very small amounts of money might be settled by a single justice of the peace. Selected by the colony's governor, justices of the peace listened to the details of these cases. Then they would decide what to do.

Sometimes merchants had to defend themselves in court. They could be brought to court if they charged too much for a certain type of product. They could also get into trouble if they took advantage of a customer's need for an item. In the Massachusetts colony, merchants were required to offer goods for a fair price. A merchant could be fined or sent to prison for not following the rules.

FOUR

The Merchant's Helpers

Whether filling the cargo hold of a ship or the shelves of a shop, the merchant depended on many of his fellow colonists. He needed goods to sell. The merchant also had to store and transport these items. In his community, he could find nearly everything he required to fulfill those tasks.

Farmers and Planters

Many merchants relied on farmers for their crops. Grains played an especially big part in many merchants' businesses. They sold these ground grains in their stores in the form of flour. Merchants also traded grain and flour with other colonies and other countries for different goods.

A merchant's store room houses the latest goods from overseas.

For the port city of Baltimore, flour became the biggest export. In the southern colonies, plantations grew tobacco, rice, and other important items for trade. Planters usually sold their crops to a local merchant. This merchant may have then made a deal with a northern merchant to send the crops to the Caribbean or London to be sold there. Much of the rice trade in South Carolina went to feed slaves in the sugar colonies of the Caribbean. In 1726, planters from South Carolina produced roughly 10 million pounds of rice.

Family Fun

For many merchants, business plodded along at a slow pace. This left them time for other pursuits. Reading became a popular pastime for some. Merchant Robert Pringle of Charleston asked several times for books in his letters to London merchants. In one note, he requested "Archbishop Tillotsons *Works* Compleat & a Book Call'd Dr. Scotts *Christian Life.*" Another person ordered the works of William Shakespeare and several books of essays from a London merchant. Colonists sometimes read stories aloud to each other during a visit.

A successful merchant might hire a music instructor to teach his children how to play an instrument. Frances Norton, sister of Virginia merchant John Hatley Nelson, wrote that music "is a very agreeable Entertainment, hope to make great progress in it having a good Ear & being very fond of it." Colonists might gather at someone's home to listen to a friend play the harpsichord, a piano-like instrument.

Barrels and Hogsheads

For shipping goods, the merchant often turned to the **cooper**. The cooper made the barrels used to transport food, dry goods, and drinks. Rum, flour, and preserved fish were commonly sold by the barrelful.

Merchants often traded goods by the **hogshead**, a type of large barrel. A hogshead could hold up to 63 gallons. These types of barrels were used mostly for liquids, but sometimes for other things. One merchant wrote that he sent ten hogsheads of Virginia tobacco to London.

To build the barrel, the cooper split pieces of wood into long strips called staves. He had to let these staves dry out for a time. The cooper then heated these strips and bent them into shape. To form the sides of the barrel, he put the staves together.

On either end of the barrel, the cooper added circle-shaped pieces of wood called headings. He also placed iron or wooden bands around the staves. These bands helped the barrel keep its shape.

Down at the Shipyard

Ships played an important role in a merchant's business. A wealthy merchant likely owned several ships of his own. He

A merchant oversees the building of barrels in a shipyard.

hired a shipbuilder to make boats that could handle the challenges of long ocean voyages.

The shipbuilding process took a long time. Most builders made only a few ships a year. To build the boats, a variety of workers took on different jobs. Blockmakers made wooden blocks used to hold ropes for the ship's sails. Another person set up the ropes, known as rigging. And yet another person made the sails.

The wood for the boats had to be left out to dry for a time. Different types of craftspeople worked with the wood once it was ready. The shipbuilder had carpenters put the frame of the ship together. Joiners built the cabins inside. Another worker made the mast to hold up the sails. And a carver made designs on some wood both inside and outside the ship.

Merchant ships needed a lot of metal items, too. A blacksmith worked with iron or copper to make parts for the boat. He created chains, bolts, and other items. The smith also provided latches and hinges for doors on board the ship.

In addition to making new ones, shipbuilders would clean up and repair old boats. They would mend any leaks they found. Sometimes a merchant's cargo could be wrecked by water seeping into the cargo hold. A busy port town might have several shipyards to keep up with demand.

Out on the Wharf

Merchants owned warehouses at the docks, and occasionally they owned an entire wharf for their ships and their goods. They held many men in bondage and in their employ to manage the flow of goods. The port city of New York, for example, was home to 12,000 people in 1740. One-third of them were African or African American, and about 2,500 were slaves serving the merchant and shipping industries.

Merchants also purchased some of the indentured servants they transported from Europe to the colonies for sale, and used them at the wharves. In port cities, there was also work for free men. When a number of ships came in, extra labor was needed to empty the ships of imports and load them with exports, and merchants hired free laborers on a day-to-day basis to do this work.

There were also the thousands of men and boys from port cities all over the British Empire, from the Americas, Europe, Africa, and Asia, who worked in the most dangerous job of the age, manning the wooden sailing vessels as they plied the waves through squalls and storms. They all played vital roles in the commerce of the empire.

FIVE

Creating a New Country

By the 1760s, the colonists clashed with the British government over taxes and over the way they were being governed. In Great Britain, a person could only be taxed by their local representative. The colonists, however, had no representatives in **Parliament**. This did not stop the British government from passing new laws to collect more money from the colonists.

Up until this time, the taxes that the British Parliament made Americans pay were customs duties and tariffs. In the 1750s, the British Empire was at war with France. Parliament needed large sums of money to pay for the war and had to get some of these funds from its colonists. By 1763, the British evicted the French from North America and split the continent with the Spanish, with the Mississippi River as a dividing line.

Angry merchants discuss tax and trade problems with England.

In order to repay creditors, Parliament raised taxes for its colonists all around the globe for the first time. The Sugar Act of 1764, for example, lowered the customs duty on British sugar to stop the smuggling of French and Spanish sugar, but the proceeds of the duty went to London to pay the national debt. Also, the Sugar Act stiffened penalties for merchants who dealt in smuggled sugar, forcing them to appear at Admiralty Courts in London, thousands of miles from home, and without the benefit of a jury. In 1765, Parliament passed the Stamp Act, a tax on paper to be paid by citizens in England and in all British colonies. This was not a customs duty but a sales tax intended to raise general revenue.

Colonists reacted strongly to these new laws. They held protests and called for a ban on British goods. The British government later decided to overturn the Stamp Act. At the same time, the government said it could make any laws it wanted in the colonies.

Trouble with Tea

A later British law lifted many of the taxes put on imported goods in the colonies. But the duties on tea remained. In fact, the British passed another law in 1773 that affected this product. The Tea Act helped the East India Company sell tea in the American colonies more cheaply than anyone else. Only a few merchants with connections to the East India Company could sell its tea, cutting out all others. Although the Tea Act actually lowered the tax on tea, cutting it in half, colonists worried that the East India Company would raise its prices once there was no competition. Moreover, if Parliament could grant a **monopoly** to a tea company, the colonists worried that this would lead to other monopolies for imported products they relied on, and that they would become dependent upon British corporations and the Parliament that supported them.

In December 1773, a ship filled with East India Company tea arrived in Boston Harbor. In protest, a group of colonists sneaked on board the ship. Among them were merchants and their employees. Merchants warned their workers that future laws like the Tea Act would strip them of their jobs. They dumped chest after chest filled with the hated tea into the water. This event became known as the Boston Tea Party. The British fought back with new laws against the colonists. One of these bills even closed down Boston Harbor for a time.

Many colonists sought a better form of government. They created a group known as the Continental Congress in 1774. Representatives from all of the colonies except for Georgia met in Philadelphia that year. The congress wrote down all of their problems with the British government. They asked the British government to fix these problems.

The congress met several times. They tried many different ways to get Britain to make changes. The congress debated refusing to let British ships bring their goods into the colonies. As one Philadelphia merchant wrote to a London merchant in 1774: "Compleat my Order as soon as Possible . . . our Congress have hinted . . . that Goods Arriving here after the 1 Decr [December] will not be permitted to be landed."

Colonists rebel against the British at the Boston Tea Party.

Time for War

The colonists tried banning British goods and blocking colonial goods from being sent to Britain. But these efforts did not help settle the conflict with the British government. Fighting broke out between British troops and some of the colonists in 1775.

Some merchants chose to fight Britain for independence. They risked losing some of their business for their freedom. The merchants had to look to other sources for some of their imported goods. Still, many merchants, such as Henry Laurens of South Carolina, believed that the Revolutionary War was necessary.

Laurens had made his fortune in buying and selling items for other people. He sold British goods in the colonies. For the colonists, Laurens found markets for their rice, deerskins, and other products. He also had friends and family living in Britain at the time. Nevertheless, Laurens disagreed with the British government about the colonies. He once wrote to his son that he wanted "to make a firm & steady opposition to the Measures adopted by the Administration for enslaving us."

Laurens helped write the first **constitution** for South Carolina. He also worked on ways to defend the state and the city of Charleston during the Revolutionary War. In 1777, Laurens went to Philadelphia to serve as the president of the Continental Congress. The congress made decisions on how to run the country during the revolution. While he was president, Laurens worked on getting the country of France to help the colonists fight against the British. The congress also worked on what later became the U.S. Constitution.

In 1780, the British caught Laurens while he was traveling to Europe. They charged him with treason, or trying to overthrow the British government. The British government ordered him to be jailed. For more than a year, Laurens remained a prisoner. The British later traded him for one of their captured military leaders in 1781.

Troubles with Trade

Some merchants had a tough time during the Revolutionary War. Trade with Britain reached a standstill, and the British navy tried to stop ships from Europe from delivering certain goods to America. Still, some of the ships were able to make it through. American and foreign merchants sneaked in much-needed guns and gunpowder for the war. In one case, they hid gunpowder from Jamaica inside hogsheads marked as sugar.

The Continental Congress even hired some merchants to get supplies for the army. In July 1775, the congress asked a group of merchants to obtain gunpowder. The merchants received a small payment for each purchase they made. The congress then requested that another group of

Merchants and other colonists took up arms to fight the British.

merchants get more gunpowder, guns, and other weapons that same year. When their money ran low, the congress used fish, lumber, and tobacco to pay for the needed goods.

In 1776, the Continental Congress called for the colonies to break free from British rule. They told the British government of their plans in a document called the Declaration of Independence. It said that "these United Colonies are, and of right ought to be Free and Independent States." Representatives from the thirteen colonies, including several merchants, signed this note.

Colonial representatives sign the Declaration of Independence.

A New Beginning

After the Revolutionary War ended in 1783, business changed for American merchants. They had once enjoyed certain benefits as colonists in their dealings with Britain and the British West Indies. Now they were part of a new nation made up of thirteen states instead of colonies.

The American government tried to make a new agreement with Britain about

School Days

The break with Britain may have affected some of the younger colonists. Wealthy merchants often sent their sons to Britain for school. They had their children educated under the care of a friend or a relative. Those who stayed at home might attend a local school or be taught by a tutor. How much education a child received usually depended on how much money the child's parents had.

Colonists did not believe that education was important for girls. Wealthy merchants would pay for a tutor to teach their daughters to read and write. The girls received instruction on how to dance and play music. They would also be expected to learn how to sew and cook. All these skills were meant to prepare them for marriage.

Their brothers, on the other hand, might continue their education in college. Some of today's most famous colleges—Harvard, Yale, Columbia, and the University of Pennsylvania in the respective port cities of Boston, New Haven, New York, and Philadelphia—were started during colonial times.

trade. It took more than a decade to complete, however. During this time, the new government worked on its own laws. Congress approved the country's constitution in 1789. It created new laws that charged duties on American and foreign ships delivering goods. Most significantly, the U.S. Congress passed a law in 1808 making the international slave trade illegal. The importation of slaves into the United States had expanded rapidly since the 1790s, and the closing of the trade was a significant economic blow to American merchants whose largest profits derived from the traffic in human beings. Some merchants continued to smuggle in cargoes of slaves from the Caribbean and Africa through the American Civil War.

Being a merchant remained a risky business. Merchants faced losing their cargoes to pirates. Bad weather at sea could destroy their ships. Even a safe arrival did not mean success. Merchants worried about selling their products in other ports. Would there be demand for their flour? Or would they have to sell it elsewhere?

American merchants rose to face these challenges. They sought to find new markets and new trading partners for goods. Traveling farther abroad, merchants found opportunities in Russia and the Far East. They brought furs, cotton, and other items to China. In return, the merchants had new wares—tea, silk, and china dishes—to sell back at home. American merchants continued to find ways to meet the needs of their customers, no matter what obstacles lay in their path.

Glossary

barter	to exchange items or services instead of using money to pay for something
bill of exchange	a letter written by a merchant promising to pay someone or instructing someone else to pay the person for the merchant
cargo	goods on board a ship
colony	an area settled by people from another country, and controlled by their home country
constitution	a written document that states how a government will be run
cooper	a person who makes different kinds of barrels
counting room	a place where a merchant keeps track of his business orders and accounts
credit	to buy something and pay for it later; also a promise of payment
duty	a tax or fee on goods
export	to ship goods out of a colony or country
factor	a person who works for a merchant
goods	items for sale
hogshead	a type of large barrel used mostly for storing liquids
import	to bring goods into a colony or country
indentured servants	individuals required to serve an employer for a set period of time
mercantilism	an economic system based on trade
merchant	a person who buys and sells things
monopoly	total control over the sale, distribution, and production of a certain product
Parliament	the English lawmaking body made up of the House of Commons and the House of Lords
piece of eight	Spanish silver coin
plantation	a large farm in the southern colonies
port	a coastal town or city where ships arrive and depart
supercargo	a person who oversees a merchant's goods during shipping
tanner	a person who turns animal hides into leather
wares	things for sale; goods

Find Out More

BOOKS

Fisher, Verna. *Explore Colonial America! 25 Great Projects, Activities, Experiments.* White River Junction, VT: Nomad Press, 2009.

Raum, Elizabeth. *The Dreadful, Smelly Colonies: The Disgusting Details About Life in Colonial America.* Mankato, MN: Capstone Press, 2010.

Sherman, Patrice. *Colonial America.* Hockessin, DE: Mitchell Lane Publishers, 2009.

WEBSITES

Colonial Williamsburg

http://www.history.org/

Take an online tour of a colonial town and meet the different types of people who lived there.

The Freedom Trail Foundation

http://www.thefreedomtrail.org/

Learn more about colonial Boston and the American Revolution by exploring the city's Freedom Trail.

Index

Page numbers in **boldface** are illustrations.

About the Author

Wendy Mead is a writer and editor. In her work, she has tackled a variety of subjects for young readers, ranging from birds to biographies. Mead has co-authored *Arizona, Utah,* and *Montana* for the Celebrate the States series. She enjoyed exploring colonial times in this book—her family came to the Massachusetts Bay Colony in 1635.

Atlanta-Fulton Public Library